ADVENTURES in HOME INSPECTION

Ronald Reagan's House

by
Jeffrey I. Charloff, P.E.. F.ASCE
Consulting Engineer

Sweet Rain Press

Los Angeles

Sweet Rain Press Regional Office: Los Angeles, California

Copyright © 2024 by Jeffrey I. Charloff, P.E., F.ASCE

ALL RIGHTS RESERVED
PRIOR PERMISSION REQUIRED FOR
REPRODUCTION IN ANY FORM

Library of Congress Catalog Card Number: 2024909069

ISBN-13: 979-8-218-41991-2

Manufactured in the United States of America

Published by Sweet Rain Press
Los Angeles, California
Visit us online at SweetRainPress.com

This book is for entertainment purposes only.

I dedicate this book to my family.

TABLE OF CONTENTS

Introduction iv

Chapter 1: *The Mysterious Telephone Call* 1

Chapter 2: *We Tangoed in the Short Negotiation* 2

Chapter 3: *A Drive to Bel Air* 5

Chapter 4: *Clues Were in the Halls* 7

Chapter 5: *Beneath the Surface* 14

Chapter 6: *Burning the Midnight Oil* 16

Chapter 7: *A Broken Promise* 18

Chapter 8: *The House Was Unveiled* 19

Chapter 9: *The Unfulfilled Promise* 20

Chapter 10: *A Personal Appeal to the President* 24

Chapter 11: *A Persistence Rewarded* 25

Chapter 12: *Closing the Chapter* 26

Epilogue 28

About the Author 36

Introduction

It was mid-year in 1986 that I found myself beginning a journey into the heart of political history. Yes, my adventures in home inspection catapulted me into a mission that awaited me when I became engaged to conduct the pre-purchase home inspection of none other than President Ronald Reagan and Mrs. Nancy Reagan. The house was in Bel Air, California which later would become their post-White House haven. As a part of this adventure that year, I continued navigating numerous corridors of Bel Air to inspect the luxurious homes of the affluent. Bel Air, as you may know, is a Los Angeles neighborhood acclaimed for its chic, posh, and private residents and residences.

Here in this text I unfold the true story of what had actually taken place before, during and after my Ronald Reagan home inspection endeavors.

Chapter 1:

The Mysterious Telephone Call

It was an unassuming June day in 1986 that I received a telephone call by an attorney who quickly established strict guidelines which he stated I must follow in order to conduct a pre-purchase home inspection for his client. He called me because I was known as being a seasoned California professional engineer specializing in high-end home inspections. Some specific parameters that I must adhere to included, for example, that he wanted me to be available on an early June date; that I spend no more than five hours maximum as a length of time at the house of interest; for me to agree to a predetermined fee he spoke of (which was in the hundreds of dollars); and, intriguingly, that I was to forego learning the identity of the buyer's name until sometime later.

Chapter 2:

We Tangoed in the Short Negotiation

During that call I communicated to him that I had conducted many home inspections for famous, important people so as to persuade the lawyer to reveal the identity of the prospective homeowner. In fact, I mentioned that I have been known in Southern California as the "Home Inspector to the Stars" as well as being nicknamed "The Real Columbo." I even named Dustin Hoffman, Barbra Streisand, Steven Spielberg, Burt Lancaster, and Sylvester Stallone as just several of my clients. But this attempt of dropping names proved to be futile. The purchaser's name he insisted was to remain shrouded for the time being. All that he could clue me in on then was that the potential buyer was a male who he described as being "more important than the Shah of Iran."

My Celebrity Clients

SYLVESTER STALLONE

BURT LANCASTER

BARBRA STREISAND

STEVEN SPIELBERG

DUSTIN HOFFMAN

I accepted the set amount of the fee which he offered me even though I indicated that my customary fee is normally a great deal more than offered for inspecting a mansion house of the grand size and lot size that he had described. I made mention of this to him because a mansion home is considered to be large in size, typically greater than 4,000 square feet, is normally stately, and is an impressive residence which takes more time to inspect. Indeed, the 6,500 square foot house size well exceeded 4,000 square feet, while I learned the home's irregularly-shaped lot was a pretty large one, being about 1.25 acres in size.

There was just one more thing in this negotiation process: I requested that whoever the unknown person who 'outranked' the shah was, I wanted to get a signed photograph of the elusive buyer – once it was eventually permissible that his client's name can be revealed. He accepted this term and I, too, was satisfied that he did so. This last piece of our negotiation concluded the completion of our verbal engagement agreement. He then furnished me with the home's address.

Chapter 3:

A Drive to Bel Air

A few days passed by and on Saturday morning I drove to Bel Air. The house was located off the westerly side of prestigious St. Cloud Road. One gained access to the dwelling itself by driving up the property's sloped blacktop driveway past the driveway entry's security swing gate to the flat portion of the property. The property's general landscaping was well–vegetated, completely absent of sparsity. The premises offered excellent privacy since one could not have readily observed the house from the street. The house was a brick house. On the east coast it would have been called an 'expanded ranch' style home, typically all on one level. This one, however, had three principal levels. Its architecture was a departure from the houses that one typically sees here in Southern California for it was mostly constructed of reported Texas-imported brick, rather than having a facade draped with stucco. The residence had a modern, mid-century feel, too. And, sure enough, it was indeed built in the middle of the twentieth century, circa 1954.

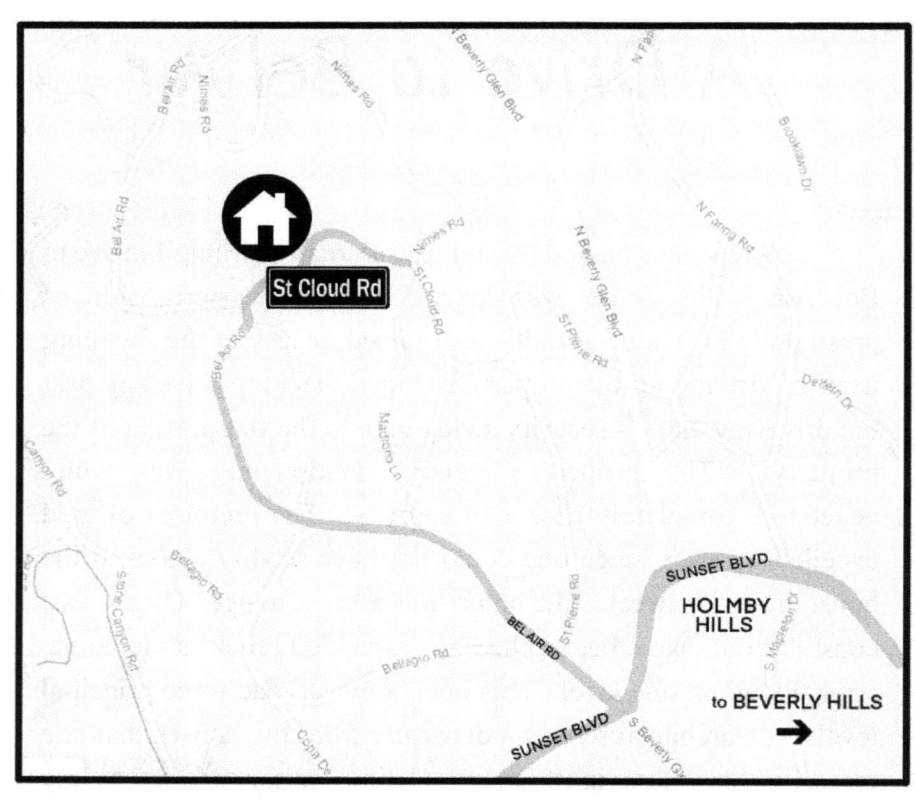

Map to St Cloud Rd

Chapter 4:

Clues Were in the Halls

As my inspection of the home's interior unfolded, pieces of the puzzle started to fall into place. Those puzzle pieces unveiled insights that this was a house not for just any celebrity, but instead, for a president. Let me tell you how:

1. A strange, but powerfully warm peculiar sensation enveloped me while I was interacting with the seller. She was an elderly woman who looked at me with inexplicable depth in a very special way. Mind you, I was asking her some pointed questions about the house. Yet, she connected with me as if I actually felt like I was Ronald Reagan himself. That feeling never came to me before, and has never happened to me since. However, this affinity was a hint that I was transcending beyond the ordinary. As such, little did I know that these initial moments in this inspection would intertwine my professional career with the highest echelons of political power.

2. The questions that I asked her took place in the home's dining room…rather, I should say, the dining

hall. I state this because the room was most spacious; it was a sprawling grand central court, and could easily accommodate a large number of occupants. This realization signaled that this was a house which had the potential to be a residence for a president. Yes, for the moment, I pictured statesmen and the elite dining while I was present inside that hall. Indeed, years later, I learned that such political notables as George W. Bush, Mitt Romney, British Prime Minister Margaret Thatcher, Canadian Prime Minister Brian Mulroney as well as German Chancellor Helmut Kohl were all visitors to the house. However, I am uncertain as to whether or not some nearby neighbors like Burt Bacharach, Elizabeth Taylor, Michael Eisner, Joan Rivers or Kenny Rogers had come by to visit – although nearby neighbor and longtime Ronald Reagan friend, Robert Stack likely did.

Political Visitors

MITT ROMNEY

GEORGE W. BUSH

MARGARET THATCHER

HELMUT KOHL

BRIAN MULRONEY

Nearby Neighbors

BURT BACHARACH

MICHAEL EISNER

JOAN RIVERS

ELIZABETH TAYLOR

KENNY ROGERS

ROBERT STACK

3. There was an uncomfortable moment, though, when I had imposed upon the seller a question as to whether the large red area rug was to remain with the house following my discovery of a cork floor the room's rug largely covered. Typically, I was aware that area rugs don't normally remain with houses upon their sale but, on account of the variety of such floor material, I wasn't sure of this. It was then that one of the seller's sons spoke up to me and forthrightly stated that he believes "the people (you represent) can afford to provide their own rug." That immediately quieted me in my interrogation upon hearing those words: "the people (you represent)." I got what he was saying. In fact, I even nodded to him and his mother that all is good so as not to instigate any trouble whatsoever between the buyer and seller. I knew I was not present for the purpose of negotiating anything out in the sale.

4. Shortly thereafter, while in the kitchen, I began to test out its aging appliances. Indeed, they were comparatively old. But, it wasn't their age that struck me; it was a connective thought that had dawned upon me. Here I was, standing in what was a seemingly aged General Electric branded kitchen. This notion led me to recall that Ronald Reagan would feel well at home here considering, in fact, that in the 1950s, he was the spokesman for the General Electric company who hosted the General Electric Theater television show. (I used to watch that classic, historical T.V.

show every week and vividly remember him always stating: "Progress is our most important product"…and I firmly believe that, in reality, these words truly fitted his belief which reflected progress and growth.) This train of thought ran through my head while I was checking out the kitchen. The General Electric brand whispered tales of Ronald Reagan's past and unearthed historical connection. Still, however, till then, I did not know who was to become the home's future occupants and political footsteps could not be traced in the kitchen with certainty.

Ronald Reagan at the Time of General Electric Theater (Circa 1953)

5. Following this room, I asked a young woman housekeeper who was present in the corridor hallway about how I could gain access to the basement. She led me to its entryway and unexpectedly told me as I began to enter it that "Nancy liked the basement." A realization echoed through the mid-century hallway and it was in that instance of time – then and there – that pure adrenaline rushed right through me. The pieces of the puzzle identifying this home's potential buyers all fell into place. I became flush with excitement and it felt as though it could not get better than this. I was experiencing a unique relief to know that the house was intended to be purchased for the Reagans as I had gotten that feeling that it was just meant to be. What this was - was an astonishing moment in my life! Just think about it…an inspection for the Reagans! Boy, does Ronald Reagan's cowboy lasso have reach!

Chapter 5:

Beneath the Surface

One of the last things I did to thoroughly inspect the premises was to crawl underneath the house into its long crawl space areas to check out the rest of the house's foundation, the structural integrity of the balance of its underfloor framing members, to look for evidence of past fires, to detect possible plumbing problems, to scour for termite damage, and so forth. But as I was crawling, I came to realize that my role transcended a standard home inspection. I wasn't merely a consulting engineer, but I was a custodian of sensitive information, entrusted with the security clearance needed to learn the close details of the Reagan residence. So, in a sense, I wasn't merely inspecting a home, but additionally distinctly and honorably selected to safeguard the foundation of a future presidential residence. The thought of this and of having been approved for this job in more ways than one made me feel good - real good.

Crawling the home's underfloor crawl space areas was the strenuous part of the physical work of the inspection, and when it was completed, I then wandered the grounds. Now that I knew who the buyers were, I visualized Ronald and Nancy sipping tea in the tea room, walking the garden, playing on the shuffleboard court, swimming in the renovated oval-shaped swimming pool, and them (or perhaps just Nancy alone) growing orchids in the orchid shed. I knew I needed to snap out of all my daydreams as I carried on to focus on the condition of the home's roof, exterior site drainage, other exterior improvements, and additional points of information the purchasers should know about.

Chapter 6:

Burning the Midnight Oil

Upon arriving home in the San Fernando Valley, I wasted no time and made it my business to transform my observations into a meticulously written report as soon as possible. The significance of doing this fueled me. And, I actually stayed up that entire night to complete it. Everything was fresh in my head. My wife, Monica, synchronized her effort and stayed up with me, too, and alongside me she typed away the 39 page comprehensive narrative report. Our combination of writing and the clattering of typing echoed our all-night endeavors. Twice or thrice was my report reviewed for any inaccuracies because I did not allow tolerance for errors. Indeed, I considered the report to be more than a professional obligation for I was crafting out a bit of history.

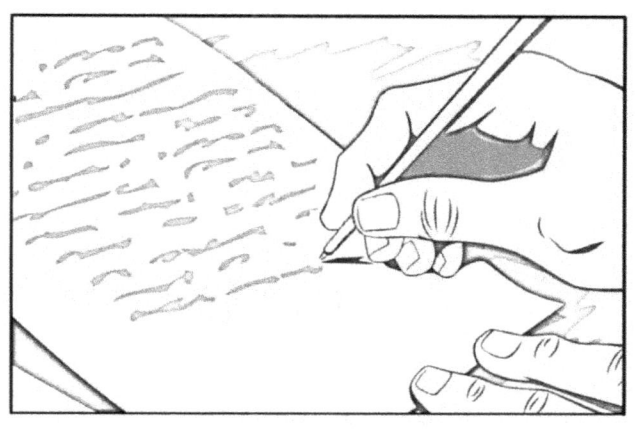

Synchronized Efforts of My Wife
Typing While I was Writing that Night

My written report was promptly hand-delivered to the law firm as I originally expressed that it would be... signed, sealed and delivered. I did not forget that in the conversation of my engagement with the lawyer who had underscored the urgency for his law firm to receive the written report ASAP.

Chapter 7:

A Broken Promise

Days later, the law firm of the 'friends of the Reagans' satisfied my account by sending me a check as payment in full for my services rendered. The financial commitment was fulfilled. However, I was not in receipt of the autographed photograph that was promised to me. Yet, I kept hush about having done this inspection as I was led to believe that that was what I was expected to do. I always uphold confidentiality, especially in the case of the U.S. President.

Chapter 8:

The House Was Unveiled

Weeks and weeks went by and the unveiling of the house purchase for the Reagans finally made headlines nationwide. It was the one I inspected. Newspapers even showed a common aerial photograph of the house.

Chapter 9:

The Unfulfilled Promise

Meanwhile, as weeks turned into more months, the anticipated photograph remained elusive. The photograph lingered as a haunting reminder of an unfulfilled agreement. Since the word was already publicly out about the house purchase, I attempted to communicate with the lawyer who had engaged me. But, by then, bureaucratic hurdles added layers of complexity toward this end for the law firm was in a state of dissolution and that lawyer who engaged me was no longer a part of the dissolving firm.

Hence, I expressed my request with one of the remaining law partners directly. I spoke very nicely to him – but he didn't exactly speak very nicely back to me. I told him that this was a term in my agreement with his law firm. But he responded in a disparaging way. Essentially he replied that if I were so interested in getting a picture of the president, then I should go to the 'five and dime' store and buy myself a photograph of the president. That upset me, but I did not argue with him, and I let this matter go.

That summer, I conducted the inspection of more Bel Air homes. One, for example, was the home of an economics professor who was selling his home and, it just so happened that this man was giving a party for the Reagans the very next day in his home. He shared this information with me after I inquired as to how he had acquired a signed photograph of Ronald Reagan that I noticed inside his living room He, being a friendly fellow, stated that he was a close friend of the Reagans, that the president frequently visited his house, and then he showed me where the president always sat around his large round dining table. Perhaps I became a bit too forward but I couldn't help resist the temptation to request if he would permit me to be seated in that dining chair just for the moment to satisfy my desire that I would be sitting in the very same chair as the President of the United States. And, yes, I sat pretty - as he had allowed me to do so!

Another house at the time which I was called out to inspect was the Bel Air home of Tony Curtis who was selling. Just as a side note, as I inspected the interior of this actor's mailbox, therein was found an invitation which had been delivered to Mr. Curtis for an event that the president was giving at the time. Well, you know, Tony Curtis being an actor as was formerly Ronald Reagan, I figured they would know each other. Maybe it was some sort of a trend in my subconscious, but as I inspected more and more houses in and around Bel Air, I noticed the presence of more and more pictures of President Reagan…and they were signed ones, too. The Reagans got around and had many, many friends. The Tony Curtis' invite was just a tiny sample of the yield of the Reagan 'reach' I experienced seeing that summer.

Tony Curtis Receives an Invitation from the President

Even one of my own friends here in the San Fernando Valley showed me the picture which he had recently received from the president. (My friend got it because he was a supporter of the Republican Party. Nonetheless, although I was happy for him, I became a bit jealous of his good fortune at the same time.) I began to think that it was I who performed the house inspection where he and his wife were going to reside; and it was I who furnished him with lots of useful knowledge about his prospective home. That should have been deemed very important to him. I even supposed how relevant it would have been to President Reagan by imagining that, if say, four reports had been simultaneously laid out for him to read at his Oval Office desk, my thought was that he just might select to pick up my report first! I then concluded that I was totally wrong to be even slightly jealous of my friend, but I instead placed blame upon myself for not having the grit and determination to insist from that law firm partner who I communicated with earlier that summer that he get me the signed photograph as I sought and which was duly promised me. I recognized that I had a plea, or better yet, I should say, I had a silent plea for a commitment which was yet unmet. My plea just lingered in the shadows.

However, there came a breaking point in my unfinished quest for the signed photo. That quest continued to develop five months later, in November of 1986. That's when I had been engaged to inspect a condominium unit for a new client of mine in the Silverlake area of Los Angeles. Two men were the sellers of their unit who walked me through their home. Again, I saw an autographed photograph of Ronald Reagan. It was sitting right there in their living room. Being inquisitive, I asked those gentlemen how they obtained it. Their reply was that they serve the president as being his cooks. This could have been my chance encounter. Their response motivated me to act.

Chapter 10:

A Personal Appeal to the President

Indeed, I did. Within me is a persistent desire for closure and to assist achieving that closure, I penned a heartfelt Season's Greeting card directly to the White House in December. Inside that card there was my expression of sincere warm wishes for Christmas greetings to President and Mrs. Reagan which later intertwined with a candid retelling President Reagan of the Bel Air inspection. I identified myself as the consulting engineer who had inspected the Bel Air house back in June and that, in doing so, besides payment, I would receive an autographed picture of the person(s) for whom I did this work for. I additionally continued to state that this was part of the verbal agreement with the lawyer of the firm that had engaged my services. But you know, I really did not truly believe that Ronald Reagan would actually receive my card, let alone read it. However, he did.

Chapter 11:

A Persistence Rewarded

Nothing happened for three years and during this time span I let go of my quest. I just didn't want the unfulfilled agreement to taunt me further. But, would you know that one winter day my wife came running up our long driveway and, almost out of breath, showed me a manila envelope having "President Reagan" printed in his handwriting on it. Not only that, but we both noticed that the envelope had been absent of stamped postage (although, instead, "POSTAGE AND FEES PAID" in tiny lettering was printed just beneath the Ronald Reagan name on this envelope). Monica must have right away guessed what was inside it, but she gave me the honor to open it up. I did so – and very carefully. And, sure enough, I received a color picture of Ronald and Nancy Reagan sitting on a white bench in their home's garden – just like I envisioned them. **"To Jeffrey Charloff - With Best Wishes"** was written on it and just below those words it was signed by him with the signature I was so familiar seeing.

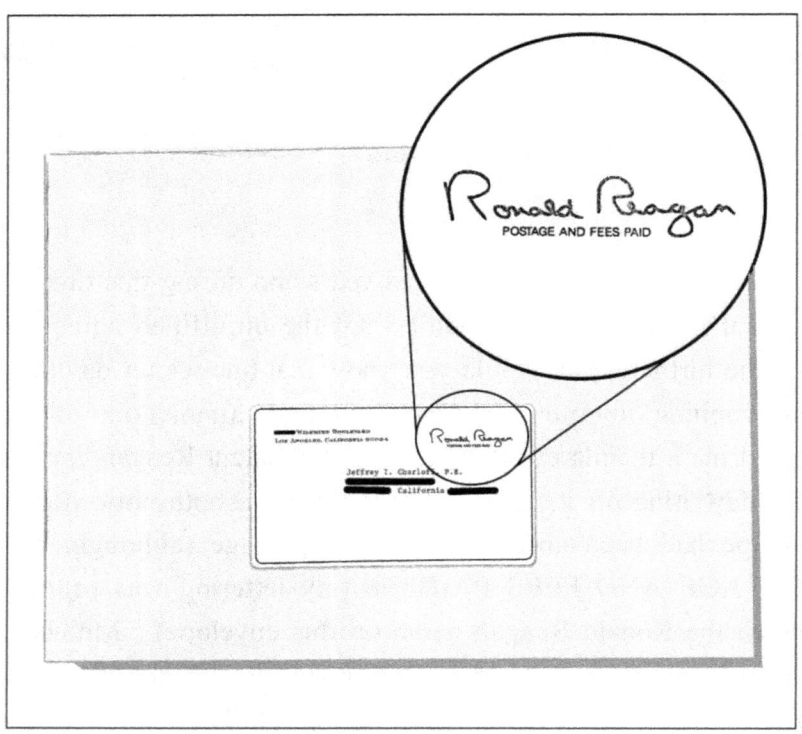

This is the Envelope that the Autographed Reagan Photo Came In

Chapter 12:

Closing the Chapter

I was amazed by this unexpected arrival of a cherished photograph! It is now my prized possession and it became a symbol of triumph to me. As such, I keep this photograph well protected because there was only one Ronald Reagan and only one Nancy Reagan – two people whom I have truly respected.

And so, I hereby need to share with you the saying that I often abide by which oftentimes helps motivate me:

> *"You can,*
> *you know you can.*
> *The question is,*
> *do you **want** to?"*

I look at this photo as a tangible proof that exerted effort, coupled with an element of luck, often begets reward. And I got what I wanted. It marked a culmination – a tiny link I feel to a chapter in American history.

Epilogue

Oh, there is just one last thing I'd like to mention which I derived as having been beneficial to my family and I on account of having done the Reagan house... and that additionally involved the work of my inspecting the Los Angeles sprawling ranch house of Frank Sinatra where I understand Mr. Sinatra had lived for more than 20 years. The latter inspection took place just months later – in January, 1987.

You see, at that time, our children were toddlers who had been sleeping in cribs all crammed up in one small room of our Chatsworth two-bedroom house. As it was, Monica and I were unsure of the timing on when we should sell our home and buy a larger home so each child can enjoy their own room. As we were in this predicament, we put two and two together and realized that, after all, the President of the United States was buying, while the "Chairman of the Board" was selling. Indeed, this answered our question for knowing good timing. Hence, we were influenced even in the timing of our decision to move.

Circa February, 1987, Monica and I went out and bought a home in Calabasas which we still reside in to this date. Surely, this was a subtle reminder of the interconnectedness of lives and destinies with theirs. Note that I unfortunately did not get a Sinatra picture which Monica and I wanted, too, but his housekeeper did give me a beige cocktail napkin marked in brown lettering "Barbara and Blue Eyes" and a paper (towel) napkin which was plain white (but of quality) having initials "FS" printed in red on it. We still keep them as a token reminder for keepsake.

Gifted Paper Cocktail Napkin and Initialed Paper Towel

And now that nearly 40 years have passed by, I can tell you that the Reagans occupied this house in retirement from 1989 until their respective deaths. He died at 93 years of age in June of 2004; and she died at 94 years of age in March of 2016. Both Ronald and Nancy died in the house.

It was the "friends of the Reagans," who had actually bought the house, and was not purchased by the Reagans themselves. That group of friends numbered about 20, some of whom were early-on political "Kitchen Cabinet members." Indeed, it was confirmed that Mrs. Reagan had been looking for a home in Bel Air for more than a year. In fact, even after she saw this house, reportedly she had in mind to view other houses as well. The price which was paid for it was $2,500,000 back in 1986. My thinking is that the purchasers believed that the price they paid seemed to be a pretty reasonable one considering the fact that an "ordinary" house in "old Bel Air" on a 1-acre parcel of land was selling for in the neighborhood of $3,000,000 instead.

Once purchased, the elderly woman seller continued to live there. She paid rent under a lease. In the year 2022, the dollar amount of $2,500,000 translated to roughly $6,675,000 or so. Note that the house had never been placed in the open market. This might have been so because I recall the seller's son had something to do with real estate. My understanding, too, is that this home was specifically given to a trust under the couple's name after they had left the White House; but the friends had gotten repaid. Nancy had the St. Cloud Road address number later changed to "668" to better suit her preferences.

Sometime after Nancy's passing, the house got sold. It was demolished around the year 2020. That marked the end of an era on St. Cloud Road. Nonetheless, the legacy of that Bel Air mansion, having been bestowed by the Reagan occupants, continues to resonate within me. It weaved itself into the fabric of history and further, into my own professional journey. Yes, I believe the echoes of this bygone era endure and is certainly a testament to the impact it had in the seemingly routine adventures in home inspection of my consulting engineering life.

Breezeway and Back Patio

Aerial View of the Bel Air Reagan House

The Reagans Sitting on a Garden Bench

So Here It Is...My Prized Possession.
It Became a Symbol of Triumph to Me.

About the Author

Jeffrey I. Charloff, P.E., F.ASCE, of Los Angeles, California is a consulting engineer since 1972 who specializes in pre-purchase inspections of residential and commercial buildings. He has conducted many home inspections for celebrities, including President and Mrs. Ronald Reagan (while in office), Burt Lancaster, Barbra Streisand, Steven Spielberg and Dustin Hoffman and is known in the Southern California region as "Home Inspector to the Stars." Since 1989, Mr. Charloff has also been a construction arbitrator for the American Arbitration Association. Numerous times he has been interviewed on national television as a structural and home inspection expert and has appeared in court as a forensic engineer. Mr. Charloff is a Fellow of the American Society of Civil Engineers, is CalEMA certified (disaster safety evaluator), and holds professional engineering licenses in the states of California, New York, and Florida.

www.ingramcontent.com/pod-product-compliance
Lightning Source LLC
Chambersburg PA
CBHW061347040426
42444CB00011B/3134